The Quick-Start Guide to Foundation Fundraising

*If you think the foundations process
is too daunting, think again!
This simple guide will help you
launch a successful foundations program.*

Jeff McLinden

With gratitude for the hundreds of men and women — and their amazing causes — I have had the privilege to serve as a consultant and friend...

...and for the friendship and partnership of those who have been my mentors for more than three decades in the profession of nonprofit development and marketing...

...AND for my wife and family whose understanding has permitted me to enjoy this profession (and the significant periods of travel and absence that have come with it).

Copyright © 2014 by Jeff McLinden

Published by CreateSpace
and Wordsmith Marketing, LLC, Colorado Springs, CO.

Copyright holder is licensing this under the Creative Commons License, Attribution 3.0.
http://creativecommons.org/licenses/by/3.0/us/

No part of this publication may be reproduced, stored in a retrieval system, or transmitted in any form or by any means, electronic, mechanical, photocopying, recording, scanning, or otherwise, except as permitted under Section 107 or 108 of the 1976 United States Copyright Act, without either the prior written permission of the Publisher or Authors. Requests for permission should be addressed to the Publisher at Wordsmith Marketing LLC, 5134 Splitrail Court, Colorado Springs, CO 80917, (719) 597-3455 or on the Web at Wordsmith- Marketing.com.

Limit of Liability/Disclaimer of Warranty: While the publisher and authors have used their best efforts in preparing this book, they make no representations or warranties with respect to the accuracy or completeness of the contents of this book and specifically disclaim any implied warranties of merchantability or fitness for a specific purpose. No warranty may be created or extended by sales representatives, sales websites or sales materials. The advice and strategies contained herein may not be suitable for your specific situation. Please consult with a professional where appropriate or to determine the best application of ideas, tactics or strategies discussed herein. Neither the publisher nor the authors shall be liable for any loss of profit, or any other commercial damages including, but not limited to, any special, consequential, incidental or other damages.

This book may appear in both electronic and physically published formats. Not all material may be contained in all formats.

The Quick-Start Guide to Foundation Fundraising

If you think the foundations process
is too daunting, think again!
This simple guide will help you
launch a successful foundations program.

Other Books by Jeff McLinden:

The Successful Development Director: How to be a SUCCESS raising friends and funds for your nonprofit organization!

The Nonprofit Communications Handbook: How to engage donors, raise more money and strengthen your nonprofit's brand through donor-focused communications.

The Christian Fundraiser's Major Donor Handbook: How to build a successful major gifts strategy for your nonprofit organization!

Partners for LIFE! Raise support for your missionary work and build a partner team for a lifetime of ministry together!

CONTENTS

Introduction	1
Are Foundations Worth the Effort?	3
Establishing Your Foundations Program	7
Research	8
File Creation	11
Cultivation	13
Solicitation	14
Measurement	17
Maintenance	21
Using Research to Shape Strategy	23
Try it...you'll like it!	24
Building your strategy from research...	27
The game is afoot...	29
Sample Foundation Correspondence	31
Sample Guidelines Request	35
Sample Query Letter	36

Follow-up Submission/Appointment	38
The Foundation Proposal	39
Sample FULL Proposal	41
The Letter Proposal…	60
Sample Letter Proposal	61
The "Application" Proposal	64
Face to Face: Presenting in Person	73
Foundation Strategy Summary	77
In Conclusion…	83

Introduction

People get excited about charitable foundations as a source of funding...especially board members. "If we could just get XYZ Foundation to give us a grant!" they say. "Why don't you send them a proposal?" Have you heard that before? Have you tried to follow their suggestion? Chances are that you failed to excite the XYZ Foundation enough to do anything more than send you a "Sorry..." letter.

There have been volumes written about grantsmanship that are voluminous, arduous, yet very helpful. And many sources exist for training in the exciting work of foundation and corporate grant-seeking. But you may be one of those who doesn't have the time or the budget to read lengthy volumes or attend expensive seminars. That's why this brief guide may be just what you're looking for.

Yes, foundation grants are sometimes difficult to win. But please note that I said "sometimes." They are far more difficult for those who don't have a clue what they're doing — yet do it anyway! The uninitiated always have more difficulty with tasks that require an understanding that there is a right way and a wrong way to be successful.

This brief guidebook is designed to help you quickly learn the right way to success in foundation and corporate grant-seeking. It is by no means exhaustive. Instead, consider it a "quick-start guide" to setting up and running a foundations program for your non-profit. I won't guarantee that you will be able to immediately claim your first $50,000 grant as a result of applying the basic principles and procedures you'll learn here. But I will guarantee that you SHOULD be able to run a tight foundations ship with every reasonable hope of successfully pursuing and obtaining multiple grants from the right foundations for your organization.

After all, that's what development boils down to: finding and keeping the right kinds of donors for your organization. In that respect, foundations are simply a special kind of donor that requires a special methodology for cultivation, solicitation, appreciation and maintenance. But successful efforts here can result in substantial lifetime partnerships that can help you advance your cause through substantial grants over many years.

That's why you should carefully apply what you'll learn here. Then you can always add to the knowledge you gain by attending grantsmanship seminars, reading books, etc.

CHAPTER 1

Are Foundations Worth the Effort?

American foundations have long been a source of significant funding for nonprofit organizations. In fact, hundreds of millions of dollars are made available to organizations like yours each year through the thousands of foundations that exist in the United States alone. Grantsmanship has become an art form that growing numbers of nonprofits do quite well – with the income to prove their expertise. But if you are planning to generate substantial portions of your annual budget through foundation grants, please know that you may be disappointed… By no means are foundations the El Dorado that will change your funding fortunes in the near term. Rather, you must be very intentional about creating and maintaining a foundation relations strategy designed for the long-term.

I once recommended to a client that they would be wise to begin a foundations program simply because they were the type of organization that would be able to successfully attract foundation support for their cause. Unfortunately, like so many others, the executive director scoffed, "I'm not going to play their games! We have needs that can't wait for those guys at foundations to play around, forcing me into their waiting games, requiring us to jump through their hoops and maybe, just maybe, giving us consideration." While it's true that foundation grants are not necessarily immediately forthcoming – and that foundations have quite strict guidelines to which applicants for grants must adhere – the same holds true for the grant-making institution as for any other type of donor: You very often reap what you sow. In other words, like all donors, it takes investment on your part to cultivate and grow enduring relationships with the right kinds of foundations before you will see substantial investment from them in your organization. My former client, like too many nonprofits, was simply unwilling to invest the time and effort.

The right kinds of foundations. That is the key to success. Far too many novices believe they can treat foundations like any other entity on their mailing list, and – in fact! – treat foundation grant-seeking like a direct mail strategy. Here's the concept...

1. Develop proposal.
2. Find foundation addresses.
3. Mail proposal to as many foundations as possible.

It's a sure-fire formula for failure! And it's why foundations are rightfully concerned about having strict guidelines for grant-seekers to follow. You must think of foundations as very particular prospective donors, with especially particular interests, priorities and rules that guide their giving. Just as you wouldn't ask the old lady down the street to subsidize your next Super Bowl party, you simply don't ask a foundation for a grant without understanding if there might be any reasonable degree of interest in your project or program. Doing so wastes their time and yours.

Of course there is potential for you to get foundation funding...IF you are careful to identify the types of foundations that align well with what you are hoping to achieve. In other words, foundation programs involve the most sophisticated marketing activity of any type of fundraising or development program you might undertake. That is why you must be willing to invest the time – and the effort – in creating, building and maintaining a foundation relations effort. There's gold in them thar hills...but you have to mine it. It won't jump out of the ground for you.

Speaking of gold, there's an old saying in the mining industry:

YOU'RE EITHER AN INCH AWAY FROM A MILLION DOLLARS – OR A MILLION INCHES FROM A DOLLAR!

Not too long ago I had a client that was successful with their very first grant request made within our carefully crafted foundation relations strategy. They sought – and were granted – a substantial, multi-year grant to help establish and fund the organization's development program, including salary, program expenses and fees and expenses for outside counsel (me!). The grant was a major boost for a small organization that needed help to gain financial independence and long-term sustainability. The total value of the grant came very close to six figures over three years. Not bad for a first effort!

Such success belies the assumption that "it takes too long, and it won't be large enough to justify the effort." Success is predicated upon careful identification of prospective foundation partners, adherence to THEIR priorities and guidelines, the proper cultivation procedures, and the right timing for the request. That is precisely how my client approached the task – and it paid off handsomely.

CHAPTER 2

Establishing Your Foundations Program

Putting together a foundations program assumes that you possess both the potential for success, as well as the desire and determination to make the effort required. The pursuit of grants can be very rewarding – as well as very frustrating! But the determination to succeed means quite simply that you are willing to invest the time to learn, to do, to learn over, and to do over, perhaps many times before you obtain your first grant. That's why I often suggest that this is a perfect arena for men or women who are process people, administratively inclined, detail driven, and meticulous in their work. If you have such a person available to you, wonderful! If not, then you might consider re-tasking someone in your organization who does exhibit these qualities. It needn't be full-time work, particularly if you are just getting started. I've had a number of clients who found an exceptional volunteer and tasked them with their foundations program for one day per week, just to get things rolling.

Where to begin? As I mentioned, there are a great many facets of foundations programs that simply boil down to one word: organization.

I always start my clients out by introducing them to six basic tasks:

1. Research
2. File Creation
3. Cultivation
4. Solicitation
5. Measurement
6. Maintenance

Let's take a look at each of these and the associated tasks...

⇒ **Research**

Too many organizations mistakenly assume that their first task is to "create a proposal." Sorry... That's not even a consideration when you're just starting to build your program. Let me define the tasks of research for you so you can begin immediately to set up your own foundations program:

1. You must research the potential areas of your organization's program that might be a good match for foundation

funding. This means careful analysis of three significant areas in which foundations may be interested

- Your <u>cause</u> – the projects and programs that are making a difference (hopefully!) for those whom you serve.

- Your <u>operations</u> – foundations are frequently interested in helping you strengthen the underpinnings of your organization, such as infrastructure, systems, facilities, etc.

- Your <u>future</u>. Foundations, like individual donors, can get excited about vision, about realizing potential, about achieving breakthroughs, about growth and expansion – if such growth and expansion will accelerate the achievement of things they value! Remember that development is not all about you and your needs. Rather it is very significantly about your donors and THEIR needs, as well.

- The purpose of this inward focus is to surface those aspects of your program AND your organization that pose the greatest potential for foundation funding. Identifying these provide the basis for your entire foundations strategy…and lead you to the next critical phase of research:

2. You must begin to identify those foundations that are the most likely matches for your organization's potential proposals – which will be based upon a prioritized evaluation of the previous step's research. As I stated earlier, the founda-

tions battles are won or lost in this phase. A huge number of nonprofits simply don't have the patience for the hours of research needed to uncover the very best foundation prospects. Ironically, more care is put into online dating quests than in foundation solicitation. Why? Because the "searchers" are looking for the "perfect match" – or as close to perfect as possible. Please hear me – your foundations activity is precisely the same! Use the tools available (see the appendix at the end of this document) to uncover the very best potential matches according to a very stringent set of criteria including:

- Stated purpose
- Areas of interest / focus
- Current priorities
- Geographic constraints or limitations
- Typical grant sizes
- Equivalent grants to other organizations
- Limitations on types of requests and/or requesting organizations
- Desired method of contact
- Proposal processes and procedures
- Timing / deadlines
- Notification processes

All of these (and sometimes more) contribute to a foundation's potential compatibility with your organization and the prospective proposals you might submit. The best part is that all this information is readily available to you. You simply need to take the time to read and evaluate the information.

If it sounds like looking for the proverbial needle in a haystack, it's not. Thankfully the tools that are available for research enable you to quickly isolate the most likely "sections" of the haystack in which to find a bunch of needles with potential. Zeroing in categories and types of foundations that have potential is like Googling keywords to produce the most likely urls in an Internet search for information. The more precise your keyword search, the fewer pages of possible links appear – until you are able to zero in on just the information you were looking for.

A variety of Internet tools and sites are available to you for foundation research, including the Foundation Center, the Grantsmanship Center and even individual searches for foundation web sites. My intent here is not to teach you how to use these tools – if you've done a Google search you already know how. Rather my intent is that you know WHY to use these tools and convince you that, without them, your chances for success at the foundations game is greatly diminished.

➡ File Creation

This second task in the foundations process is equally important. Setting up your administrative systems will not only increase your effectiveness – it will also greatly increase your efficiency. Don't simply keep an electronic record of prospective foundations and try to operate that way. Rather you will want to create a specific filing system for your physical foundations files. And those files will provide you with both a prospect management system and a partner tracking system for your foundations efforts.

Your efforts in this area, you see, will generate many types of hard-copy correspondence, activity reports, proposals, follow-up reports, tracking of financial history, etc., than is typical for any other type of donor. At the same time you will be storing the foundation's current guidelines, contact information, lists of board members, annual reports, and other information including press clippings, articles, etc., that help provide insights for your cultivation and submission plans.

Creation and maintenance of these files will help you manage future prospects, current foundations in your proposal pipeline, past foundations from which you received grants (and want to seek future grants) and foundations that have turned down previous requests. Creating such a management system will save you, literally, hundreds of hours of work in the long run trying to remember the myriad details involved in creating and maintaining good and healthy foundation relationships.

What should go in the file? Here's a list:

- Basic foundation information summary (see appendix)
- Copy of most recent annual report

- Copy of most recent Form 990 (the IRS requires foundations to file this form annually to detail the grants made by the foundation in that tax year. Their 990 is one of the best ways to see the recipients of grants and the amounts awarded).
- Copy of all correspondence you initiate (guidelines requests, query letters, proposals submitted, follow-up letters, thank-yous, etc.)
- Copy of all correspondence the foundation initiates (guidelines, acknowledgment of submission, status of submission, rejection letters, notification of grants, etc.)
- Record of activity
- Copy of any requested or promised reports to the foundation regarding your use of funds awarded, documentation of impact, results, etc.
- Notes from meetings, phone calls, presentations, etc.
- Cumulative record/report of all grant activity.

As much as we all want to save trees and store everything electronically, that is simply impossible to do with a thorough foundations file!

Cultivation

The last section has already given you a good indication of what is involved in cultivation of foundations. However, unlike working with individual donors, it involves a process largely dictated by the individual foundation and laid out in their "guidelines for submission." The guidelines specify how, why, when, where, who, and how much. They make no guarantees. But they expect adherence or you can expect rejection.

Let me add, however, that foundations are made up of people. And people, ultimately, are the decision makers at foundations. Thus, you should make every attempt to cultivate relationships with contacts you are able to identify at the foundation. Board members. Program officers. Contact people. Administrative assistants. Trustees. There are many options. You need to start somewhere. And your research will help you. Be sure to bring your list of potential contacts to your board meetings to see whether there might be any links among your members. It's surprising how often you'll find connections in what you would think are the most unlikely places!

Your cultivation activity will include a variety of efforts – including personal correspondence (to request guidelines, annual reports, etc.), phone calls (to request appointments for a visit, ensure receipt of proposal submissions, etc.), personal visitation (for friendly "get to know you" visits, presentations, etc.). But the frequency and timing are very much in the control of your prospective foundation "targets." You must make the effort – repeatedly – in order to move the relationship forward. That's what cultivation is all about.

➡ **Solicitation**

The foundation proposal is the most common instrument for obtaining a grant. The length and depth of a good proposal vary dramatically – and, again, it is most often determined by the target foundations, themselves. Guidelines for grant requests are quite specific bout the process AND the format they desire for your grant requests. You will soon discover that the larger foundations with extensive staff and regimented processes tend to require more detailed, formal proposals. These proposals can be quite extensive with pages upon pages devoted to identifying the problems, research completed to address the problems, descriptions of projects or programs to the most minute details, complete budgets, timelines, accountability plans, follow-up plans, etc., etc. If you want a taste of this type of proposal, take a look at the requirements for USAID grant requests (USAID is the United States Agency for International Development).

Smaller, family-run or private foundations may be substantially less demanding, often asking only for a "letter proposal" that describes the project or program, its objectives and costs, the people involved and the timing for funds needed. That can be accomplished in a two-page letter – and, indeed, foundations often request that your proposal not exceed two pages. The norm is somewhere in between these extremes. If you're like most of my clients, you'll find your proposals will typically fall in the range of five to eight pages. This is enough to identify the problem you are wanting to address, describe the solution you are proposing, provide the details to demonstrate how your solution will ultimately achieve your objectives, provide the evidence that will validate your ability to complete the task, provide any pertinent details that will be helpful (such as budgets, additional funding sources and plans, etc.) and make the request for partnership. Strangely, that simple progression pretty well defines the outline of any proposal you may create. In slightly different terms you should plan your proposal like this:

1. Problem Statement
2. Proposed Solution
3. Description of Project, Program or Service
4. Expected Impact
5. Verification of Effectiveness
6. Budget / Funding Sources
7. Funding Request

The sample proposal I've included will show you how this basic outline is followed when crafting the proposal. And the foundations you approach will appreciate the degree to which your proposal anticipates and answers the kinds of questions they would ask you. That's the value of having a basic outline that progresses naturally from the big picture (problem statement) through the solutions and the details of how their prospective grant will be used to carry out your solution. It isn't difficult to put together good proposals... It simply is an exercise in good communications – having your information well planned and presented – and providing compelling reasons why the foundation should consider your request.

⇒ Measurement

If this seems like an odd inclusion in the foundations process, chalk that up to thirty years worth of an almost insane focus on measurement! You certainly want to record and track the pertinent data that surround your efforts to secure foundation grants. Not only for the sake of your program, but also for the sake of those foundations that are "on your list." Here's why:

1. First, you want to keep very good records of the foundations you approach AND the ones you decide aren't a good fit for your organization. This will save much unnecessary and repetitive work by others who may follow in your footsteps.
2. Second, you need to track every interaction you have with those foundations you are cultivating, including the rejection letters, the maybes, the changeover in personnel, etc. The more you know, the better your chances of creating excellent matches with foundations, creating enduring relationships with their staff members, and maintaining productive relationships as far as grants are concerned.
3. Third, your measurement of RESULTS is imperative to convey to the awarding foundations the impact of their grants. Like all donors, and maybe even more so, foundations are greatly concerned with their own financial stewardship – and if you can't point to positive results as a consequence of their giving, you will not continue to receive grants. It's just that simple.

Keep meticulous records. Measure results. Report those results. Period. By the way, below is a sample of a simple report to help you keep track of your foundation activity:

Foundation Name	Location	Closing Date	Anticipated Grant	Category	Date Expected	Likelihood	Status	Grant Rec'd	Amount
America Development Fndn	Alexandria, VA	None	25,000	Medical Assistance	9/2/09	90%	A		
Action Aid Fndn	Washington DC	6/10	35,000	Orphan & widows	9/2/09	85%	B		
Rotary Fndn	Evanston, IL	None	50,000	Disaster Relief	12/2/09	100%	A		
Procter and Gamble	Cincinnati, OH	None	25,000	Feeding & Poverty	12/2/09	100%	C		
François-Xavier Bagnoud Fndn	New York, NY	None	15,000	Disaster Relief	12/2/09	85%	A		
Newman's Own Foundation	Connecticut	7/2	10,000	Children & Hunger	1/1/10	85%	D	X	10,000.00
Borden Foundation	Columbus, OH	12/2	25,000	Feeding & Poverty	3/16/10	90%	B		
Huston Foundation	St. David's PA	12/2	10,000	Community Development	3/15/10	50%	D		
Avon Fndn	New York, NY			Women, health, emergency					
United Airlines Fndn				Disaster Relief					
American Express Fndn				Feeding & Poverty					
Astrozeneca Pharmaceuticals				Product donations - Africa					
TOTAL			$ 195,000					Total Received:	$10,000.00

STATUS KEY
A = File Created / Guidelines Requested
B = Query Letter Sent
C = Appointment Made / Presentation
D = Proposal Submitted

Here is another sample for you that is an example of how you might keep track of all activity with a particular foundation.

International Child Care **Foundation Contact Summary**

FNDN Name	**Chatlos Foundation**
Address to:	Mr. William J. Chatlos, President The Chatlos Foundation, Inc. P.O. Box 915048 Longwood, FL 32791-5048
Contact:	Mr. William J. Chatlos, Pres. Alice E. Chatlos, Chairman of Board & Sr. Vice President
Average Grant	$25,000 - 50,000
Interest Areas	Religious causes (evangelical), medical and health related concerns
Deadlines:	Only one grant in 12 month period... resubmit six months after denial; no deadlines, but see guidelines for specifics.
Project	CBR - Santo Domingo -- $25,000 -- UNFUNDED UCH - Port-au-Prince -- $25,000 -- UNFUNDED

Priority 1
State
Telephone 407-862-5077
FAX

Proposal Date:
1st: 4/2/96
2nd: 12/6/96
3rd: 7/1/97

Amount Requested 25,000   **Amount Received**
Date Promised   **Date Received**

Date of Contact	T	V	L	Purpose of Contact / Persons Contacted, Etc.
4/2/96	X	—	—	Called for clarification in guidelines... need U.S. office and program budget for project request.
4/2/96	—	—	X	Sent initial "preliminary" request with exec. summary of CBR program.
4/8/96	—	—	X	Acknowledgement of proposal... Preliminary Review Committee meets in May. Notification of any additional info for next full meeting. (Letter signed by Wm. J. Chatlos)
5/28/96	—	—	X	Denial letter for this proposal... signed by Carol J. Chatlos, sec'y.
6/14/96	—	—	X	Sent letter requesting clarification about proposal -- not interested in this specifically or may
6/18/96	—	—	X	resubmit in six months? Received reply from Wm. Chatlos... May resubmit or new request.
8/30/96	—	—	X	Sent copy of Summer 96 GRACE w/letter -- intent to resubmit.
11/20/96	—	—	X	Sent copy of Fall GRACE and GCH brochure... Submit proposal in 2 weeks!
12/6/96	—	—	X	Submitted proposal for UCH for 25,000
12/15/96	—	—	X	Confirmation of receipt... Prelim review in Jan... Etc. -- I sent thank you on 12/23
1/20/97	—	—	X	Denial Letter for this proposal. Responded with thank you and intent to submit in six months.

This simple sheet was created by a client using a simple database program with a format that made keeping track of all foundations activity very simple, easily "updatable," and easily sortable by any of many important criteria, such as submission date, status, grant range, etc. It is a relatively simple matter to set up something like this -- and an invaluable method of keeping track of your activity with a single foundation AND your entire foundations target base.

Finally, you should definitely use a good battery of reports to measure the impact of your foundation efforts. Every software program has some type of reporting package that can help you do this. But you may wonder which types of reports are the best to use.

Your donor management software can likely provide a variety of reports that will help track progress with foundations, both for contact and foundation relationship management and for tracking financial performance. These include the following types:

Action Reports:

1. Tickler and Action Detail Report
2. Action Summary Reports

Profiles, Lists and Directory Reports:

1. Constituent Directory
2. Organization / Constituent Profile

Financial Reports:

1. Constituent Giving History

Analytical Reports:

1. Solicitor Goal Summary
2. Solicitor Performance Reports
3. First/Greatest/Latest Report
4. LYBUNT Report (Last Year But Unfortunately Not This)
5. Top Donors Report

Maintenance

This sounds so janitorial! But the success or failure of foundations programs is a direct result of two things: persistence in pursuing the right foundations and acute attention to maintaining excellent relations with those you pursue.

Repeating what I mentioned in the last few paragraphs, foundations have a financial responsibility just as you do. Their success in accomplishing the purposes for which they exist is, in part, dependent upon your success in achieving results with the grant monies they entrust to you. It is a delicate – and vitally important – relationship. Don't screw up by failing to communicate. Failing to visit. Failing to report back. In other words, treat foundations as the unique type of donors, partners or friends that they are.

Be sure you do not miss critical deadlines – either for submissions or for reporting results. Be sure you remember that the principals of your foundations are PEOPLE – and they like to be treated as such. This goes beyond mere maintenance – it becomes a matter of special cultivation and attention to the same kinds of concerns that your other major donors experience in their lives. Success here can create friends for life – that's the mark of a successful foundations program.

CHAPTER 3

Using Research to Shape Strategy

In the last chapter I said that successful foundations strategy begins with research. In this chapter we'll take a look at how this works. Unfortunately too many new development directors get discouraged that they can't succeed simply by mailing out proposals to every foundation they can find. On the other hand, perhaps this is fortunate after all — because it means that people like YOU who approach the foundations process correctly will actually advance closer to the head of the line!

So where do you begin? Ultimately you are looking for the proverbial match between your organization and a group of foundations that share your enthusiasm for your cause, project or program. It is a matter of shared values — and, fortunately, there is plenty of public information to help you determine whether there is a possibility of that your values line up with the foundations you are researching.

Back in the day (meaning pre-Internet), you or your associate would spend hours in a Foundation Center Library poring through directories, reading annual reports, viewing aperture cards, reviewing selected foundations' Form 990 filings, and taking voluminous notes. Or you would purchase massive (and expensive) Foundation Center directories for each year's updated records of those organizations that were somewhat aligned with your organization's niche (for example, "Religion" was a directory that contained profiles of every foundation in America that made grants for religious purposes — admittedly an extremely broad category!).

Today, however, the process is extremely easy simply because this information is now online, in a variety of forms and sites, and is instantly searchable by entering the right keywords in Google. A side benefit to online access is that you can access individual foundations' websites directly to obtain their most recent guidelines, giving priorities, forms 990, professional staff listings, board member information, etc. For those of us in the profession who've been around awhile, such information availability is heaven!

Try it...you'll like it!

The best way to understand the power of research is to try it for yourself. So here's your assignment: Let's pretend you are an organization that is interested in improving digital literacy among underprivileged youth in North Carolina... Let's see what we can find that could lead us to a prospective foundation relationship:

When you Google "charlotte foundation grants for literacy" some 655,000 results are displayed. Wisely, you look at page 1 to see what might jump out. And, amazingly, the top spot is held by the John S. Knight Foundation, the legacy of Knight Publishing Corporation which owns newspapers across America.

```
Google   charlotte foundation grants for literacy

         Web    Images    Maps    Shopping    More ▼    Search tools

         About 655,000 results (0.31 seconds)

         Knight Foundation Grants Support Charlotte Literacy and Educatio...
         www.knightfoundation.org/.../knight-foundation-grants-support-charlott... ▼
         Mar 22, 2000 - Knight Foundation Grants Support Charlotte Literacy and Education.
         MIAMI – Reach Out and Read, a national early childhood literacy initiative, ...

         BOBCATS: Bobcats Charitable Foundation - NBA.com
         www.nba.com/bobcats/charitable_foundation.html ▼
         The Charlotte Bobcats have formed a new philanthropic initiative by creating the ...
         Through grant awards with a strong commitment to the areas of literacy, ...

         Dollar General Literacy Foundation Grant - CMS School Web Sites
         schools.cms.k12.nc.us › CMS School Web Sites › Crown Point Elementary ▼
         Sep 13, 2013 - Tina Mohrman, Literacy Facilitator, Received a $2,000 Grant from the
         Dollar General Literacy Foundation Grant to support Crown Point's ...

         NCDPS - At-Risk Youth Grants
         www.ncdps.gov › Sections › Juvenile Justice › Grants and Funding ▼
         The American Legacy Foundation offers grants to reduce tobacco use by youth.
         The focus is on the Charlotte-Mecklenburg area. .... The purpose of this fund is to
         provide local literacy programs throughout the U.S. with books and other ...

         Dollar General Presents $72500 in Grants to Charlotte-Area ...
         newscenter.dollargeneral.com › News ▼
         Oct 12, 2013 - Dollar General Presents $72,500 in Grants to Charlotte-Area ... school
         received a $2,500 grant from the Dollar General Literacy Foundation.

         The Barbara Bush Foundation offers grants for literacy programs ...
         www.examiner.com/.../the-barbara-bush-foundation-offers-grants-for-lit... ▼
         Jul 23, 2011 - Nonprofit organizations in Charlotte can apply for The Barbara Bush
         Foundation for Family Literacy grant. Organization that work to increase ...

         FUNDING OPPORTUNITIES - BOOST Collaborative
         www.boostcollaborative.org/fundingopportunities ▼
         The Charlotte Martin Foundation Youth Grants The Charlotte Martin ..... Is your high
         school ready to start a financial literacy program? Discover has the grant for ...
```

Clicking to the foundation's site reveals everything you need to know -- "about the foundation," "what we fund," "funded projects" and more. A quick scan reveals hundreds of grants made to unrelated projects and programs, however a search for "digital literacy" in their keyword-driven "Find Projects" box brings up several recent projects. You can also view their professional staff and board of trustees to look for any existing relationships you might have.

But the real meat and potatoes of the site (and every foundation's website) is their grant guidelines and application page, PLUS their online financial records — that all important Form 990 — that is the source of information to guide you in crafting your proposal. You see, the information in the 990 tells you not only who received grants from the foundation in the particular year you're looking at, but you can get a good sense of the SIZE of the grants and the specific purpose for which the grant was given. Take a look at the photo to see what I mean.

NORTH CENTRAL TEXAS COUNCIL OF GOVERNMENTS FOUNDATION 616 SIX FLAGS DRIVE ARLINGTON, TX 76005	NONE	PUBLIC CHARITY	TO BUILD SOFTWARE TO HELP LOCAL LAW ENFORCEMENT AGENCIES COLLABORATE WITH NEIGHBORHOOD CRIME	47,500.
OHIO & ERIE CANALWAY COALITION 47 WEST EXCHANGE STREET AKRON, OH 44308	NONE	PUBLIC CHARITY	TRUSTEE-ADVISED GRANT (CRUTCHFIELD): FOR EXTERIOR SIGNAGE AT THE OHIO & ERIE CANAL NATIONAL HERITAGE	15,000.
ONE LAPTOP PER CHILD FOUNDATION 222 THIRD STREET, SUITE 0234 CAMBRIDGE, MA 02142	NONE	PUBLIC CHARITY	TO CONTINUE THE TEST OF ONE LAPTOP PER CHILD AT HOLMES ELEMENTARY SO THAT THE SCHOOL SYSTEM HAS MORE	240,000.
OPA-LOCKA COMMUNITY DEVELOPMENT CORPORATION 490 OPA-LOCKA BOULEVARD, SUITE 20 OPA-LOCKA, FL 33054	NONE	PUBLIC CHARITY	TO CELEBRATE THE ART OF THE AFRICAN DIASPORA BY PRODUCING A MULTIDISCIPLINARY JURIED ARTS FESTIVAL	60,000.
OPEN KNOWLEDGE COMMONS C/O BERKMAN CENTER FOR INTERNET AND SOCIETY, 23 EVERETT STREET, 2ND FLOOR CAMBRIDGE, MA 02138	NONE	PUBLIC CHARITY	TO INCLUDE KNIGHT-COMMUNITY LIBRARIES IN THE CREATION OF A NATIONAL DIGITAL LIBRARY	990,000.

You'll need to scroll a bit to find this section of the 990, but you'll learn much!

Building your strategy from research...

Information is a powerful tool to help you shape your own strategy for each foundation you target. Using the example above, you would need to ask yourself a number of questions that would help you determine your course of action:

1. Is there a good fit between the objectives of the foundation and my organization's cause/programs / projects?

2. Does their grant history show a track record of giving to similar projects as the one I have in mind?

3. Do their current grant-making priorities fit with my array of potential projects to present?

4. What is their grant-making cycle? Do I have time to fit into their current year's deadlines?

5. Who are the best contacts for me to correspond with for my initial communications and to get into their process (more information about this in the next chapter)?

6. Can I arrange a friendly visit to get to know their staff — and to get on their radar screen?

7. What would be the best timing for me to discuss a possible proposal?

8. What is their average *initial grant amount* so I can structure my proposal and my request appropriately?

9. Do they require an *application,* a *letter proposal,* a *summary proposal,* or a *full proposal* when the time comes?

10. Am I <u>committed to a long-term development</u> process with this foundation?

The final question is, perhaps the most important one you must ask yourself. Because the work involved in building and maintaining a solid relationship with foundations is substantial enough that you *cannot be casual about it!* If you are not willing to work hard for the privilege of creating and keeping a major foundation partner, then you should think hard about approaching them at all!

As you may have surmised your *strategy* with an individual foundation is very similar to your work with individual major donors. Each has its own set of values that drives giving behavior. If you fail to recognize this, then you fail, period. Whether it is the largest, corporate-based foundation or the smallest family-based foundation, you must be willing to recognize their preferences, follow their desires and their processes, and to treat them as valued <u>partners</u> in the work you are doing. With the very first contact you make, you are entering into a delicate dance of relationship development that can be mutually-beneficial. But it takes time and care. As a friend likes to say, you don't get pickles by squirting vinegar on cucumbers!

The game is afoot...

Searching for and researching individual foundations is an interesting "treasure hunt," but it can be a bit cumbersome and time consuming compared to using the tools designed specifically for foundation research. Let me focus on just one: Foundation Directory Online, which you'll find at foundationcenter.org.

While this online directory is a paid service, it is well worth the relatively small investment you'll make to have its robust search tools at your disposal. While Foundation Directory Online offers multiple monthly subscription levels (starting at less than $200 per year), for about $1000 per year you'll have a professional level tool that provides you easy access to more foundation information than you can possibly imagine and the search tools to narrow your results to the explicit results you are seeking. Believe me, the time you save is well worth the cost — and the potential you'll uncover for partner foundations will be well worth the investment.

In the previous chapter I mentioned that some liken foundation research to the proverbial hunt for a needle in a haystack. The tools available to you change the game in your favor.

CHAPTER 4

Sample Foundation Correspondence

As stated previously, there are a variety of communications that will occur between you and your foundation prospects. These include several fundamental types:

- The Guidelines Request
- The Query Letter
- The Submission Letter

Guidelines Request Letter

Often the foundation will want to limit the amount of information they must deal with in order to make their funding decisions. That's why it's imperative that you understand their guidelines before you submit ANYTHING to a foundation! Violate their guidelines and you'll never – repeat, NEVER! – have an opportunity with that foundation. Remember the Golden Rule: He who has the gold makes the rules!

While many foundations are now publishing their guidelines on their websites, you must be aware that the guidelines often change. So it is a good idea to request directly a current copy of the guidelines so you're playing by the right set of rules. Besides, this simple correspondence is one way to establish a stream of communications between you and the foundation – and, ultimately, that's precisely what you want.

The Query Letter

Please don't discount the importance of this critical step! This is where so many organizations are simply too eager and jump the gun, sending a proposal that has NOT been agreed to by the foundation. The query letter is very similar to permission marketing – it changes the relationship. Unsolicited grant requests are like e-mail spam – and they are treated as such by most foundations.

When you determine from a foundation's guidelines that there may be a good match, it is ALWAYS best to submit a query letter that points out the potential match and requests further discussion to determine the foundation's interest. In other words, you are seeking permission to initiate the proposal process. It's the first real step toward building a relationship with the decision-makers at the foundation.

The Submission Letter

You'll note from the last of the sample letters below, the submission of a proposal follows the invitation from the foundation to do so. And this usually occurs after there has been discussion about the nature of your project or program, ideally in the form of a face-to-face appointment. By the time you have reached this stage, there has been a healthy amount of back-and-forth communication between you and the foundation – and you have begun to build a good file on your interactions with the foundation being careful to document the things you have learned, the people you have connected with, the flow of communications and their outcomes, etc.

This is the *process* of foundation relations… and it is one of the reasons that those who have patience and persistence do better than those who expect foundations to be a "money pump."

I've noted earlier that there is a great deal of administrative work involved in a successful foundations strategy. That's why it is usually helpful to have someone with strong administrative skills involved in this type of work. Someone who has great organizational skills, who is organized, and who is a strong communicator. Following the *process* is critical to success – so you need someone who is *process oriented* to manage this stream of communications for ALL the foundations that are prospects for your organization.

On the pages that follow are samples of a simple guidelines request, a query letter and a submission letter designed to accompany a formal proposal. Styles will differ, but the idea is to have something to act as a model to guide your own correspondence.

Sample Guidelines Request

October 14, 2012

Becky Wilder, Administrative Assistant
The ABC Foundation
West Wilberforce, PA 11111

Dear Ms. Wilder,

I am writing to request a current copy of the ABC Foundation's guidelines for grant applications, as well as a copy of your most recent annual report, if available.

Child Care Outreach International is a health and development agency that works to bring health and wholeness to needy families and children, primarily in Haiti and the Dominican Republic. Our work includes the only pediatric hospital in Port-au-Prince, as well as community-based health programs focusing on both urban and rural populations in both countries. I would very much like to learn more about the ABC Foundation's funding priorities for this year, as it seems that we might have common interests and that there is good potential for partnership.

I would be most grateful if you could forward the materials to me at the address below. Thank you for your help. I look forward to hearing from you.

Sincerely,

Jack Johnson
Director of Development

Sample Query Letter

January 29, 2013

Mr. Ted Williams
The ABC Foundation
West Wilberforce, PA 11111

Dear Mr. Williams,

I am writing in hopes that the ABC Foundation might entertain the possibility of partnership with Child Care Outreach International in a project of great importance to suffering and needy children and families in Port-au-Prince, Haiti.

Child Care Outreach International is a health and development agency that works to bring health and wholeness to needy children and families, primarily in Haiti and the Dominican Republic. Our work includes Children's Hospital, the only pediatric facility in Port-au-Prince, as well as community-based and church-based health programs focusing on both urban and rural populations in both countries. For 30 years CCOI has worked at the prevention and treatment of diseases that contribute to one of the world's highest rates of infant mortality.

Your stated interest in providing assistance for children in Third World countries leads me to hope that you might favorably consider a request for much needed support for an initiative we are launching to stem the causes of suffering and death among 50,000 of Haiti's poorest residents. Called "Urban Community Health," the program is an innovative community-focused program designed to attack the root causes of illness, suffering and death among thousands of Haiti's poorest inhabitants, particularly young children. Like most of our programs, this UCH program is run by and for nationals in the poorest slums and shanty towns of Port-au-Prince, with limited access to health care and limited resources to pursue treatment.

Children living in Cite' Je're'mie and similar slums are among the most susceptible to communicable diseases that are always serious -- and often deadly. Malnutrition, diarrhea, typhoid, tetanus and, especially, tuberculosis are perpetual enemies whose effects are multiplied in the crowded, unsanitary environment. UCH workers have targeted 20 communities for child and adult vaccination programs, door-to-door child health visitation programs, nutrition education, family planning education, community sanitation efforts and clean-water programs, as well as literacy training for community members. The goal is to build community awareness of, and responsibility for, individual and family health.

It is our desire to build on several years of initial success with the UCH Program and work during this year to reach a population of 50,000 individuals. The ABC Foundation is one of several we are asking to help make this possible in partnership with Child Care Outreach International.

The UCH Program represents one of our highest priorities, with its success contributing greatly to improving infant and child mortality in the crowded slums of Haiti's capital city. I would like to talk with you about the potential for partnership with the ABC Foundation to bring healing and hope to these needy families. I will call within the next week to see if a phone appointment can be arranged.

Thank you for your time and consideration. I look forward to speaking with you.

Sincerely,

Jack Johnson
Director of Development

Follow-up Submission/Appointment

May 3, 2013

Mr. Ted Williams
The ABC Foundation
West Wilberforce, PA 11111

Dear Mr. Williams,

I am pleased to submit a proposal to the ABC Foundation for program partnership with Child Care Outreach International in our Urban Community Health Program. This is a unique, community-based approach to prevention of disease and promotion of good health among the desperately poor inhabitants of slum areas in Port-au-Prince, Haiti.

You will note that we are asking the Foundation to consider a grant of $24,128 to help fund expansion of the UCH Program to a target community of 50,000 people. We are pleased that you have agreed to a visit by Dr. John Smith, ICC's Haiti-based executive director, who will be able to answer any questions regarding the program and our proposal. I confirmed this morning with Ms. Becky Wilder his intent to meet with you at 10:00 a.m. on Tuesday, May 25, before he heads back to Haiti.

Enclosed you will find all the pertinent documents requested in the Foundation's Guidelines, as well as a brief Case for Support describing Child Care Outreach International and its programs.

Thank you for your time and consideration.

Warm regards,

Jack Johnson
Director of Development

CHAPTER 5

The Foundation Proposal

As I've said, proposals can take a variety of forms. Much depends upon the individual foundation and their specific guidelines or requirements. Your best bet is to find out exactly what the foundation expects from you and others who are seeking grants.

Follow the process outlined later in the chapter called "Foundation Strategy Summary" and you'll have a good chance of matching your organization to the foundations that make the most sense – and who MAY be interested in your project or program. When it comes time to prepare your proposals, think about developing several models that will work for a variety of purposes, such as a "letter proposal," an "executive summary," a "full" proposal or a "full-blown" proposal.

On the next several pages you'll find a sample proposal that fits into the middle of the pack. While not as detailed as some, this could be categorized as a "full blown" proposal by many standards.

This was prepared to find funding for a medically-oriented program for community health development in a foreign country. Consequently, there is quite a bit of detailed information, typically required by the types of foundations that support such programs. This sample will give you a good idea of the type of information that CAN be required to satisfy the needs of your prospect foundation.

Not all will require the level of detail provided here. This is why it is critically important to understand fully just what are the specific requirements of your target foundation. And, ideally, you can confirm those details when you visit the foundation *and they invite you to send your proposal!*

Sample FULL Proposal

Urban Community Health Program

A program to help treat and prevent disease
through loving outreach and service
among desperately poor and needy children
in slum communities of Port-au-Prince, Haiti

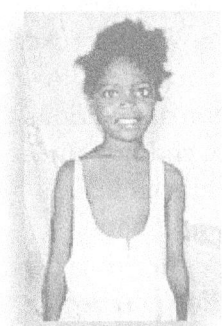 

A Proposal for Program Partnership
to
The ABC Foundation

Childcare Outreach International, Inc.
3620 Broad Street
Anytown, OH 43214

555-447-9952   Fax: 555-447-1123

Urban Community Health Program

A program to help treat and prevent disease among desperately poor and needy children in slum communities of Port-au-Prince, Haiti

EXECUTIVE SUMMARY...

Haiti is the poorest nation in the Western Hemisphere, indeed, one of the world's most needy and poverty-stricken nations. Life for children in Haiti is very tenuous, with most suffering needlessly from malnutrition and various communicable diseases. In fact, one in ten children under age five die from such diseases, of which tuberculosis is the most significant. The crowded slums and shanty towns of Port-au-Prince, Haiti's capital, are rife with such disease due to overcrowding, poor sanitation and very poor nutrition.

Child Care International's Children's Hospital is located near several of these slums and serves a clientele comprised of thousands of poor and needy families. In an effort to control the spread of disease, and to eradicate the factors which cause so much pain and suffering, the Hospital has launched an <u>Urban Community Health Program</u> designed to foster sound health practices within the slum communities themselves. UCH workers have targeted 20 communities totaling 50,000 residents for child and adult vaccination programs, door-to-door child health visitation programs, nutrition education, family planning education, community sanitation efforts and clean-water programs, as well as literacy training for community members. The goal is to build community awareness of, and responsibility for, individual and family health.

Haiti has suffered terribly during the last several years due to political instability and a shattered economy resulting from the U.S. embargo, which was in effect until President Jean Bertrand Aristide was returned to power in October 1994. Recovery has been painfully slow, with the majority of Haiti's poor still struggling to find employment, and thus, enough food to feed their families. The Children's Hospital, and Urban Community Health workers, have seen a significant increase in children suffering severe malnutrition, which exacerbates the increase of communicable diseases. As a result, the Hospital's caseload of both inpatients and outpatients has increased due to rising hardships -- such as extreme crowding and severe contamination of water -- experienced in the slum communities. Thus it is imperative to not only continue, but to increase the disease-prevention / health-promotion efforts being targeted at slum populations through the UCH program. These same priorities have also been identified as high-priority health concerns for Haiti by the World Health Organization.

Child Care Outreach International is seeking funding partners to help the Urban Community Health program expand its services, meeting the needs of the full 50,000 target population during the 2006 and 2007 calendar year.

<u>We are asking the ABC Foundation to consider a grant of $24,128 to help make possible the Urban Community Health Program through 2007.</u>

Project Information and Objectives...

"Expansion of Child CareOutreach International's Urban Community Health Program"

A community-based program for the treatment and prevention of disease among desperately poor and needy children in slum communities of Port-au-Prince, Haiti.

The Problem...

As in many third-world nations, the children of Haiti face each day with uncertainty. For the poorest families, their children's survival is very much in doubt. The ravages of poverty, malnutrition and disease contribute to one of the highest child mortality rates in the world. One in ten Haitian children do not live past the age of five, victims of serious diseases like tuberculosis, typhoid, and diphtheria. Thousands die each year from effects of malnutrition, especially diarrhea-induced dehydration, the leading cause of childhood death. Tuberculosis is the second-leading cause of infant and child death. In contrast, child mortality in the United States is 12 deaths among every 1,000 children. For Haitians, the real tragedy is that such high rates are preventable -- if children can only receive the type of care and medicines they need.

Haiti is the poorest nation in the Western Hemisphere. Troubled by political and social turmoil, especially during the last several years, the Haitian populace is also crippled by economic poverty and ignorance of common health care practices that can preserve their children's health. As a result, disease strikes hard and often -- with few or no resources available to pay for medical treatment at government clinics and hospitals.

The Program...

Meeting the needs of children in such conditions, and showing them love and hope, is the reason for Child Care Outreach International's existence. But, after thirty years of service in Haiti, we've discovered that real progress cannot be made unless attention is given to disease prevention as well as to disease control. Prevention must happen at the community level, which requires a mobilized effort beyond the walls of existing institutions. That is why the <u>Urban Community Health Program</u>, an extension, or outreach, of our pediatric care facility, Children's Hospital, was born.

The <u>Urban Community Health Program</u> (UCH), is an effort to help strike at the root of the problem within the crowded shanty town and slum districts surrounding the hospital. Cite' Je're'mie is one such slum, its air acrid from the stench of rotting garbage mixed with animal and human waste. Here people live in shacks and shanties crowded next to a deeply rutted, mud "road" encircling the slum. Some of these homes are made of cinder block, or of old boards slapped together with nails and rope. Some have walls of cardboard with corrugated tin roofs. A few are made entirely of flattened tin cans riveted together.

There are no trees here to shade these homes from the boiling Caribbean sun. Temperatures inside are sweltering during the heat of the day. Flies and mosquitoes have free access through open doors and windows, as well as the gaping cracks in every wall. When it rains, sewage contaminated water can back up to a depth of four feet, flooding homes with filthy water, and threatening little children who generally sleep on floors. Children living in Cite' Je're'mie and similar slums are among the most susceptible to communicable diseases that are always serious -- and often deadly. Malnutrition, diarrhea, typhoid, tetanus and, especially, tuberculosis are perpetual enemies whose effects are multiplied in the crowded, unsanitary environment. Child Care Outreach International launched its initial effort to help these children and their families in 1989, targeting an area of about 4,000 people for its Urban Community Health Program. Today UCH has expanded to 50,000 people with a focus on three key areas in order to reduce the incidence of disease and death:

- Restoration of Health through Intervention;
- Promotion of Health through Prevention;
- Empowerment for Health through Education.

The target population is the focus of <u>immunization programs for little children and young mothers</u>... <u>Nutrition education programs</u>... <u>Pre- and post-natal care and training programs for pregnant women</u>... <u>Training, equipping and certification programs for traditional birth attendants</u>... <u>Distribution of Vitamin A to reduce childhood blindness</u>... <u>Programs to build latrines and develop potable water supplies</u>.

Most significantly, the UCH program focuses efforts on mobilizing volunteers and workers <u>from within the communities themselves</u> and on literacy training to help create a sense of self-determination for the residents.

Education is a critical part of UCH and Children's Hospital, with families participating in a variety of programs including daily devotions, literacy training programs for community workers and families, reproductive health clinics, as well as basic health and nutrition training. The combination of these efforts is having a significant impact for large segments of the population in and around Port-au-Prince, as the combined programs of Urban Community Health and Children's Hospital touch some 170,000 individuals annually.

<u>Project Management and Supervision</u>

The UCH program has grown from targeting five slum communities within Port-au-Prince during 2004 to 20 neighborhoods in 2006-07 including the neighborhoods of Je´re´mie, Yenyen, Cayes, Siclait, Des Jeunes, Delmas 33, De´livrance and thirteen more with a total population of some 50,000 individuals.

The community activities are coordinated through a partnership of 16 ICC "health agents" who work within each community to identify several "volunteer collaborators." This produces a network of trained and trusted community workers who visit homes, regularly monitor children's and mothers' health progress and coordinate community education and training programs, including "mothers' clubs" providing basic child-health instruction.

Each agent reports to a program supervisor under the direction of Dr. Francisque Villineuve, a Haitian medical doctor responsible for the general implementation of the UCH program. General direction of the program is overseen by Dr. Renée Lestrand, M.D., M.P.H., the longtime director of Children's Hospital. Dr. Lestrand received her medical training at the National University of Haiti and her masters in public health at Johns Hopkins University. She has more than 20 years of service at Children's Hospital, and understands well the value of community-based health promotion/disease prevention.

While Haiti is the object of attention for some 300 organizations around the world, there is generally no one else working within these desperately poor slum communities to help get at the root of health and disease problems that fester there. Child Care Outreach International is the logical agency to carry on this type of activity in the communities that surround our most visible and recognized work at Children's Hospital. Child Care Outreach International's thirty year history of service in Port-au-Prince, plus our staff consisting of 99% Haitian nationals, has earned the trust of the families we are serving, thus enhancing our success rate in a culture that is tired of having things done for them, rather than with them.

UCH Program Budget and Funding...

The budget for the Urban Community Health program for 2006-07 is $172,704 (for detail, see attachment). This comprises 21.5% of the total budget for Children's Hospital programs, and represents a very favorable program cost of under $4.00 per individual served in the target area. The UCH budget is supported by funding raised from various sources, including designations of individuals, churches, agencies and foundations. The United States Agency for International Development provided 2004-05 funding support for the program, but eliminated all support for UCH in 2006 due to budget revisions.

We are requesting a grant of $24,128 to help with the UCH program in 2007, which represents 14% of one-year's project budget. If the ABC Foundation is pleased with the results of the program we would hope you might consider renewing partnership in subsequent years to help maintain a course of program expansion.

Sources of funding and requests for partnership in the program are as follows...

World Health Organization -	$ 13,988	(8.1%)
A.O.P.S. -	$ 46,961	(27.2%)
U.S. and Canada donors -	$ 21,473	(12.4%)
Christoffel Blindenmission -	$ 26,807	(15.5%)
Government of Haiti -	$ 23,333	(13.5%)
World Bank -	$ 16,014	(9.3%)
	$148,576	
Funding remaining -	$ 24,128	(14%)
	$172,704	100.0%

CONCLUSION...

We respectfully request that the ABC Foundation consider this strategic opportunity to significantly impact thousands of Haitian children and families who struggle for hope in their daily battle against poverty, malnutrition and life-threatening diseases.

Your participation will have a dramatic effect, not only upon their health and well-being through the UCH Program, but on their hope for a secure future for their children. <u>The cost of Urban Community Health is very favorable, with a significant return on investment</u> -- <u>a full year's health intervention and preventive, as well as clinical care, at a cost of just $4.00 per individual</u>. As Child Care Outreach International has this opportunity to bring both healing and hope to needy children and families through Urban Community Health and Children's Hospital, the partnership of the ABC Foundation with Child Care Outreach International can help make a dramatic -- and significant -- difference in their lives.

Thank you for your consideration.

Urban Community Health
Operating Budget: 2006-07

The Urban Community Health program represents 6.5% of the total Child Care Outreach International budget, including all field and headquarters expenses. Below is a summary of both the United States Headquarters operating budget and the UCH program budget.

	UCH Program	U.S. Headquarters
Human Resources	121,142	99,148
Supplies	12,433	1,900
Transportation	5,512	3,820
Facilities & Utilities	3,761	19,329
External Services	16,098	17,203
Program Contribution		43,998
Total Operating Expense	158,946	185,398
Buildings	0	0
Furniture & Fixtures	1,537	0
Equipment	3,996	2,000
Vehicles	0	0
Total Capital Expense	5,534	2,000
Total Program Expense	164,480	187,398
Fundraising Expense (5%)	8,224	
TOTAL NEEDED:	172,704	

USA Budget Allocation

U.S. Budgeted Income:	897,502
U.S. Budgeted Admin. Expense:	(187,398)
represents 20.9% of total	
U.S. Budgeted Fundraising:	(57,750)
represents 6.4% of total	
U.S. Net to Field Programs:	652,354

General Information...

1. ORGANIZATION...

    Child Care Outreach International, Inc.
    3620 Broad Street
    Anytown, OH 43214
    (555) 447-9952 • Fax: (555) 447-1123

    Please contact: Jack Johnson, Director of Development

2. BACKGROUND...

    Child Care Outreach International is a health development agency operating in Haiti since 1966 and the Dominican Republic since 1988. The organization is working to change the conditions that make people poor, sick, hungry, unemployed and afraid. The organization pursues the need for both an immediate, compassionate response to human suffering as well as for long-term solutions to the root causes of blockages to human development. All programs function under the authority of an International Board of Directors comprised of members of three legally recognized National Boards which oversee the organization's national offices in the United States, Canada and Haiti.

Child Care Outreach International is recognized as a leading agency in dealing with health issues in Haiti, often partnering with the World Health Organization and other international health organizations. The staff of approximately 285 persons works under the direction of Dr. John Smith, M.D., an American medical doctor based at Children's Hospital located in Port-au-Prince, Haiti. Fully 98% of Child Care Outreach International's field and program staff are Haitian or Dominican by nationality, with many medical staff completing their training in both U.S. and Haitian or Dominican universities.

Key Staff include the following individuals:

Dr. John Smith, M.D.	--	Executive Director
Dr. Renée Lestrand	--	Director, Children's Hospital
Mrs. Marie Benoit	--	Director of Operations, Haiti Programs
Mr. Charles Joiner	--	Controller
Mr. Jack Johnson	--	Director of Development

The Child Care Outreach International Board is composed of three bodies with members representing the United States, Canada and Haiti. The entire board meets twice annually. The U.S. Board also meets twice annually as a separate body.

Child Care Outreach International Board members are:

Dr. Charles Bigbucks, Dallas, TX	--	President
Mrs. Hope Lotsadollars, Irvine, CA	--	Vice President
Mr. Kiefer Johnson, Chicago, IL	--	Treasurer
Mrs. Betty Wilson, Denver, CO	--	Secretary
Dr. Wilfred Anderson, Landover, MD		
Rev. Jack Morningstar, Columbus, OH		
Mr. Harold Boerner, Pittsburgh, PA		
Mrs. Stella Dallas, Springfield, IL		
Mr. John Davidson, Springfield, OH		
Dr. Jeff Morehead, Boston, MA		

No members of the board are employed by the organization. All members serve without compensation. Board members are eligible for partial reimbursement of travel expenses related to Board business, but most consider such expenses part of their personal contribution to Child Care Outreach International's work. All staff, field and management tasks have been delegated to the Executive management team under the direction of Dr. John Smith, who is employed by the Board. This proposal has been authorized by Dr. Smith with the understanding of the Board that the primary task of fund raising is charged to the staff team.

3. FINANCIAL INFORMATION...

Child Care Outreach International programs benefit from various sources of funding from the international community. The organization has been the recipient of grants from private and public foundations, churches, missions organizations and individuals. Income is classified into three categories:

a) Individual Donors/Churches;
These are the backbone of Child Care Outreach International's financial base, contributing an average of 38% of the total income annually.

b) Foundation/Agency Grants;

These organizations are viewed as significant partners, contributing an average of 25% of total annual income. Some partnering organizations include:

- United Methodist Committee On Relief (UMCOR)
- The Kellogg Foundation
- The Bethesda Foundation
- The Branscombe Family Foundation
- The Canadian Public Health Association
- Christoffel Blindenmission, Germany
- Tear Funds (U.K., Holland, Belgium)

c) Government / International Agency Funding.
Because of the severe nature of human suffering in Haiti, partnering government and international agencies have contributed significantly toward programs, about 27% of total income. Government agencies are changing international policies and reducing such efforts. Child Care Outreach International in 2005 created a resource development function in North America and is working to expand national donor bases in order to replace such government funding. Partnering agencies include the following:

- The United States Agency for International Development
- The Canadian International Development Agency (CIDA)
- CEBEMO/MEMISA
- World Health Organization

* NOTE: Funding from U.S. government agencies represented only 11.1% of total financial support.

The remainder of income is a combination of in-kind donations, including medical supplies, drugs, vehicles and equipment, as well as minor fees charged for certain adult treatments and sale of tuberculosis drugs to other organizations.

Where Child Care Outreach International's Income Goes...

	2006	2007	2008
Program Services			
Haiti	79%	78.4%	79%
Dominican Republic	6%	6.1%	6.1%
Fundraising/Admin	15%	15.5%	14.9%

[NOTE: While the name of the organization and names of individuals associated with the organization have been changed, the proposal here is an actual proposal that was successful in securing the funds for the program described.

Again, not all proposals will require the degree of detail provided here, but this is an excellent example of the various elements that may be required when you approach foundations for grant consideration.

The author of this proposal gave permission to reproduce it here for you.]

The Letter Proposal...

Often the foundation will want to limit the amount of information they must deal with in order to make their funding decisions. In such cases you may be asked to submit a "letter proposal" summarizing your request for a grant. These are often the most difficult to prepare, for it requires careful writing and editing to reduce the elements of your project or program to two pages! Of course, this is just the front end of the process – your foundation prospect will want more detail IF they decide your letter is interesting enough to warrant further investigation.

On the next few pages is a sample of a letter proposal so you can see how you might prepare your own:

Sample Letter Proposal

January 29, 2013

Mr. Ted Williams
The ABC Foundation
Suite 100, Harrison Building
100 Main Street
West Wilberforce, PA 11111

Dear Mr. Williams,

      Thank you for your invitation to submit a brief proposal so the ABC Foundation might consider partnership with Child Care Outreach International in a project of great importance to suffering and needy children and families in Port-au-Prince, Haiti.

      Your stated interest in providing assistance for children in Third World countries fits very well with an initiative we are launching to stem the causes of suffering and death among 50,000 of Haiti's poorest residents. Called "Urban Community Health," **the program is an innovative community-focused program designed to attack the root causes of illness, suffering and death among thousands of Haiti's poorest inhabitants, particularly young children.** Like most of our programs, this UCH program is run by and for nationals in the poorest slums and shanty towns of Port-au-Prince, with limited access to health care and limited resources to pursue treatment.

Children living in Cite' Je're'mie and similar slums are among the most susceptible to communicable diseases that are always serious -- and often deadly. Malnutrition, diarrhea, typhoid, tetanus and, especially, tuberculosis are perpetual enemies whose effects are multiplied in the crowded, unsanitary environment. UCH workers have targeted 20 communities for child and adult vaccination programs, door-to-door child health visitation programs, nutrition education, family planning education, community sanitation efforts and clean-water programs, as well as literacy training for community members. The goal is to build community awareness of, and responsibility for, individual and family health.

> It is our desire to build on several years of initial success with the UCH Program and work during this year to reach a population of 50,000 individuals. The ABC Foundation is one of several we are asking to help make this possible in partnership with Child Care Outreach International.

For 30 years Child Care Outreach International has worked at the prevention and treatment of diseases that contribute to one of the world's highest rates of infant mortality. The UCH Program represents one of our highest priorities, with its success contributing greatly to improving infant and child mortality in the crowded slums of Haiti's capital city.

> On behalf of the Board of CCOI, our medical staff in Haiti, and the needy children and families who could benefit so greatly from this program, **I am asking the Foundation to consider a grant of $24,128 to help fund expansion of the UCH Program to a target community of 50,000 people who will be reached in the last six months of 2008.**

Specifically, these funds would make possible the expansion of door-to-door visitation by trained medical staff to evaluate and prescribe the types of medical assistance that could save thousands of children's lives. Funds provided would add twelve trained health workers in addition to providing the medical supplies needed for diagnosis and basic treatment of the most common conditions found in Cité Je´ré mie and other targeted communities.

I am hoping we might count the ABC Foundation as a strategic partner in helping these needy children and families in one of the poorest nations on Earth. Thank you for your time and consideration of this proposal. Please let me know if I can provide any additional information that will help you and the ABC Foundation board make a funding decision.

I look forward to hearing from you soon.

Sincerely,

Jack Johnson
Director of Development

The "Application" Proposal

Many foundations prefer to eliminate to standardize their submission process to make their job of evaluating funding opportunities more uniform. They require that you submit your proposal according to a specific application-style format. This tends to cut down a bit on creativity, but also on verbosity that tends to creep in when proposal writes wax eloquently about the merits of their project or program!

It is challenge for many proposal writers to summarize their projects in short statements that fulfill the requirements of an application, but it can be done so your proposal meets the foundation's application guidelines and still provides a comprehensive picture of your organization and the value of the specific project you are proposing. On the following pages is an example so you might see what to expect.

As with previous proposal samples, names and other information have been altered and the proposal used with permission.

BELIZE CITY TRAINING CENTER
Cross-Borders Friendship Services

Project Budget: US $ 270,000 ($ 155,000 has been raised for this project)
Amount Requested: $37,000

Contact Information:

Frank Thomasson, Executive Director
Office: (XXX) XXX-XXXX   fax: (XXX) XXX-XXXX
Cross-Borders Friendship Services
2222 Delmonico Avenue, Vista Grande, CA 92432

1) Organizational Background

Mission

Cross-Borders Friendship Services was founded in 1983 to serve poverty-stricken people in Central America. Our purpose is "to assist people in Central American nations by developing public benefit services for people in need." Cross-Borders also works cooperatively with other nonprofit organizations seconding relationships or internship opportunities for staff members of those seeking to establish work in our areas of service.

Track Record

Since 1998, when the governor general originally invited us into Belize, our work has grown considerably — today we have twenty-eight foreign staff and over thirty local Belize staff working in Belize City within many segments of the local community and government. Our local staff are crucial to impact the communities in which we serve, and their training and development (in both job and leadership skills) is one of our highest priorities. Hence the need for the Belize City Training Center, to provide a location where even more ongoing training can be provided, both for our U.S. staff, and for those coming from the local community.

Our intention has never been to provide what "Belize needs," but instead Cross-Borders staff members have worked with local agencies to determine how our available resources and skills can be used to address locally-identified needs. This cooperative approach has helped build strong relationships with all levels of society in the local area and throughout the nation. We have received advice, encouragement and help from the Provincial government, local churches and many local community organizations. Many local officials have asked if they can join Cross-Borders when they retire — a rare open door of trust that would never have happened apart from Cross-Borders' unique approach.

Leadership

CEO: Frank Thomasson – EMBA Rutgers University (2005), BA Mount Union College (1977), 11 years with Cross-Borders in Belize.

Board members:

Chairman – Dr. Bill Chitwood (Executive Dir Osteopathic Foundation Colorado Springs)

Vice Chair/Secretary – Dr. Mary Peacock (Chair Intercultural Studies – Texas Christian University)

Treasurer – Mr. Thomas Farmer (Controller – Salem Aeronautics, Oregon)

- Mr. Don Miller (Vice President – Brandeis University)
- Mr. Charles Monk (President – Monk Engineering, Philadelphia, PA)
- Dr. Dave Hopkins (Pastor – Calvary Baptist Church, Ft. Wayne, IN)
- Mrs. Lynnette Tonkins (CEO, Wimbish, Inc., Canton, OH)
- Mr. Vernon Stambaugh (Missionary/Field Chairman in Central America (17 years)

Staff: Twenty-eight International staff and seven more candidates scheduled to arrive in Belize in the next 12 months. Some 30 local paid staff work within various projects in Belize.

Programs

Cross-Borders is in three main geographic regions in Belize (population 334,000).

- <u>Belize City</u> – English classes for medical, government and local professionals; assist a local orphanage with training of their staff; handle all provincial government relations; host some 200-300 international visitors each year; work with local churches on a weekly basis with many of their social programs.
- <u>Belmopan</u> (23,000 people) – Community center with a computer lab and library for local young people; doctors work alongside local doctors in the county hospital three days each week.
- <u>Dangriga</u> – (rural district) – Agricultural training; medical clinic and local public health workshops.
- <u>Work in all three regions</u> — professional young people through family, business and personal development lectures; help local school teachers.
- <u>10 villages surrounding Belize City</u> – working with local infectious disease and public health departments on SARS, rickets, and other critical health issues for the area.

Government Agencies
- Public Health Bureau – teach Family Practice medicine at the provincial medical school and bring in medical experts from all over the world for short training sessions.
- Education Bureau – teach English teachers in five rural counties for one week at a time with 50 to 120 teachers attending.
- Public Security Bureau – Conduct ethics and values training conferences for Belize's national police force.

2) Current Need

The current need is for a centrally located Belize City Training Center and office facility to better support our strategic purposes. This will allow Cross-Borders to help build capacity, increase credibility with local officials, and leverage new opportunities for expansion of services. We currently operate in a residential area that is difficult to find, which does not inspire official confidence in our ability to grow local and nationwide services.

Changes in local officials and the expansion of our work into new locations require that we develop a more visible service presence in Belize

City. Our official status necessitates that the Cross-Borders facility be moved to a non-residential location that is easy to find and visible from the street. Our current location lacks space to properly entertain local officials or for support of internal training and administrative functions.

Over the last several years, Cross-Borders' staff have developed a unified conviction that the future of Cross-Borders's ministries in Belize City will center around training: the training of our own staff to serve in their areas of expertise within the Belize City community, the training of local staff and volunteers, and capacity building training to disadvantaged members of the local community. Because of this, the desired new facility will be called the <u>Belize City Training Center</u>.

3) Meeting the Need

A facility for the proposed Belize City Training Center has been found. On October 18, 2013, local staff discovered a nearly completed building in central Belize City. We are preparing to purchase a 360m^2 suite (three times the size of the current location) within a new 19-story office building situated next to a major intersection. The building has parking, is convenient to Belize City's main north-south transportation artery, has great bus connections, and with a small guest apartment downstairs — very useful for our heavy visitor load. The space will be divided into multiple hard-wall offices, a separate reception area, a language tutoring room, a conference room, and a large multipurpose classroom, which will comfortably hold 80 people. This larger classroom will greatly enhance our ability to provide training programs the community desires.

4) Measurements of Success

Cross-Borders focuses on 4 Key Results Areas (KRAs). All of them will be used in measuring the success of this project as indicated in the chart below...

Key Results Area (KRA)	How the Belize City Training Center will impact the KRA
Sustainable Skills Transferring skills and resources for economic and social sustainability	• Provide a center for the local sale and marketing of local craft initiatives, as well as a center for providing financial counsel to project participants • Training young rural workers in a locally owned orphanage • Ongoing English language training for local residents • Family Practice medical training lectures to local and regional doctors
Leadership Training Equipping local citizens with leadership skills and experience	• Provide, on a regular basis, marriage and family seminars in cooperation with local churches • Staff training (in service) program for Cross-Borders' 30 plus Belizean workers
Involved Community Reflecting the integration of Cross-Borders with the local community	• Annual Cross-Borders Introduction Day for local and national officials in the following bureaus: Public Security, Religious Affairs, Civil Affairs, Foreign Affairs, Belize Charities Foundation, and Poverty Alleviation • Provide English training to new strategic sectors of the local community including: translators for the various city and provincial government trade and foreign affairs bureaus; disadvantaged rural school teachers; young people. • Community medical clinic; Consulting work, and all the current Belize City projects, which would continue but *continue under one roof* with the Belize City Training Center • Hold Summer English Day Camps for local children

Delighted Partners	• Host the Belize City Foreign Fellowship on a weekly basis (40+ people)
Our interaction with visitors, supporters, organizational partners and sending organizations should *delight* them	• Host monthly in-service and appreciation days for all Cross-Borders local workers • International office functions • Hosting of some 140 short-term visitors annually

5) Estimated Project Expenses

The total cost to purchase the office space and complete the build-out is $270,000. Of that total, $206,000 is needed for the purchase on March 1, 2014. The balance will be used to finish and equip the empty shell.

6) Funding

At the beginning of this project (July 2013) Cross-Borders had already saved $50,000 in anticipation of such an opportunity. Since then, we have received another US $105,000 in contributions. As a result, $155,000 is earmarked towards this project with another $51,000 needed by March 1, followed by $64,000 needed by June 1.

7) Sustainability

Analysis has shown that operating costs will be virtually the same as the existing office. Also, because this is a property purchase in a quickly-rising real estate market, we protect our overall sustainability in Belize City.

8) Organizational Finances (audited financials will be mailed separately as requested)

	2013 Actual	2014 Budget
Income	$1,805,745	$1,888,734
Expense	$1,515,679	$1,817,068

9) Summary & Conclusion

Cross-Borders Friendship Services' dream is to create sustainable social services projects that provide long-term benefit to the people of Belize and surrounding regions. This means we must train and equip more local staff and volunteers to be passionate, dynamic leaders who can impact their nation through a self-sustaining service ethic and growing concern for their fellow citizens. Cross-Borders' proven record of working to impact this region can be further enhanced through the purchase and completion of the Belize City Training Center.

The ABC Foundation's investment of $37,000 will help ensure that these goals can be reached by providing space for training that will significantly impact Belize for years to come. Thank you for the opportunity to present this proposal. We look forward to your partnership.

Hopefully these samples of actual proposals can serve as a helpful model for your own. Proposal development is not terribly difficult, but it is exacting, sometimes tedious work to craft model proposals for your projects and programs that can then be adapted to the various requirements of the foundations you choose to target. Once you have the model, however, that adaptation can be accomplished quite quickly and easily permitting you to build a significant list of active foundation prospects with proposals in their respective systems.

CHAPTER 6

Face to Face: Presenting in Person

If you've spent any time in nonprofit resource development, then you already know that the most powerful fundraising approach is face-to-face solicitation [If you DON'T understand this, then I encourage you to read my book, *The Successful Development Director*]. This is a fundamental principle that applies to any type of fundraising -- including working with foundations.

I can't stress enough that establishing personal relationships is at the heart of successful cultivation and solicitation. And nowhere is this more important than with those prospective MAJOR partners you're asking to invest significant contributions to your cause. So you must remember that foundations are not some "money pump" with anonymous decision makers waiting to dole out grants. Most foundations you will encounter have a staff of some sort -- large or small -- that plays a key role in influencing directors decisions regarding whom to fund. Not to mention board members, themselves, who have responsibility for stewardship of the foundation's considerable assets.

Cultivation of relationships with any or all of those affiliated with your target foundation is one of your most important objectives, beginning with the office staff, the executive director and, if possible, one or more board members. And, as a good friend is fond of saying, "Nobody ever got milk from a cow by mailing it a proposal. You've got to get up close and personal and stroke, stroke, stroke!"

Quite simply, this means making the necessary appointments to get to know the foundation and its people. And often this will result in your being able to make a personal presentation either as a prelude to an invitation to submit a proposal, or giving you the opportunity to present your proposal in person.

Either way, you have a unique chance to have a significant influence on how your proposal will be acted upon by the foundation. So it is essential that you be prepared to "sell" your project or program in such a way that it becomes a no-brainer for the foundation's decision process. In this regard, let me simply say that you will never succeed if you adopt the mindset that the pursuit of foundation grants is simply about you getting grants from foundations. Rather, it is about creating positive (and ongoing) relationships with foundations that are *mutually beneficial*. That is to say, there is as much value for the foundation as there is for you and your organization!

It is in the *personal interactions and presentations* you share with foundation personnel that helps underscore that you are equally as interested in *their* benefit as you are in your own. That you desire them to feel they are making a sound investment that will help accomplish their purposes and objectives as much as your own. Without a focus on how to create value for the foundation, you might as well hang up your strategy and go home.

This book is not the place to deal with the psychology of donor behavior, but it is an important topic for your study. Similar to individual donors, foundations hate to "be sold." Rather, they prefer to "buy."

So, what is it that they are buying? Ultimately, only three things:
- Good feelings
- Solutions to problems
- Seizing of opportunities

While these general principles are extremely helpful, the fact is that you won't get far without understanding the individual motivations – call them values, if you like – of those on whom you will be calling. That's why it is important to understand that the real issue for you in working with those within the foundation is concentrating on relationship development. Getting to know the person – NOT just their potential! And don't forget that, as individuals, your foundation contacts have their own ideas, interests, and involvements that play a significant role in influencing their decisions.

This is not intended to be a motivational book. But many a funding battle has been lost due to donor reps who have lousy outlooks on life, poor attitudes about their organization, an aversion to human interaction, or are simply sourpusses. There are lots of words to describe these types of people – my friend and former boss Larry Johnston tells of "those who have the gift of enlightenment: they can light up a room just by leaving."

Suffice it to say that you MUST be enthusiastically supportive of your organization's work – in other words a "passionate professional" in representing your organization to others. You should exhibit...

- An Attitude of Expectancy...
- An Attitude of Trust...
- An Attitude of Enthusiasm...

And you should realize the power that emotion has in your presentations to donors. While many admire stoic, emotionless logic in "professional" presentations, the truth is that, while logic makes people think, emotion is what makes people act. If you can't be genuinely passionate about the opportunities you present to donors, then you might consider an alternate career in the food service industry.

CHAPTER 7

Foundation Strategy Summary

I know, I know... You're thinking, "I appreciate the content in this guide, but it's an awful lot to remember. Can't you help me with a "cliff's Notes" version that won't involve all the thumbing back and forth through this book?

But, of course! On the following pages is the essence of foundations strategy summarized into the critical steps you should follow to establish a successful foundations department. Simply follow the steps and you will discover that including foundations in your development operating plan is not daunting. And it could even translate into serious grant money coming your way to advance your cause. A word of caution, however... Remember that foundations are just as interested in being involved in QUALITY endeavors, just like anyone else who gives to your organization. So begin with a solid objective to fund a solid project or program. Then follow these steps:

1. **Research:** Using the Foundation Directory, Internet resources, individual foundation Web sites or other reference works available, you would obtain the addresses and contact names of foundations that would appear to be interested in the work of your organization. A master list can be made and a contact form made out for each foundation in order to track both communications and responses. A good step to begin with "targeted" foundations is with the "request for current guidelines" letter.

2. **Query Letter:** The directories generally give a good idea of how to approach specific foundations, what the initial contact should be, etc. If appropriate, using the information on contacts, write a query letter to see if the foundation would consider a proposal from you. The information you glean from the directories may indicate whether a proposal summary would be appropriate at this time. If not, include it anyway.

3. **Follow-up Phone Call:** Indicate in your letter that you will call within the next week to see whether the foundation is interested in your proposal. For local foundations, or those within the areas of planned visits to other donors, it would be appropriate to ask whether you might make an appointment for a personal visit to explain more about your organization's plans.

4. **Visit:** If you obtain an appointment, that is the time to explain a bit of your organization's background, as well as your own. Be sure you understand going in what their interests are and focus on the types of related opportunities within your organization's portfolio that would pique their interest and involvement. Be prepared to outline what you will accomplish with funds raised. It is also appropriate to utilize your general

Case for Support (if you have one!) as a reference tool during the presentation, and as a leaving piece.

It is absolutely critical that you are prepared to talk in detail about specific plans/activities!! It is also vital that you ask them to please consider your request for funding!! Only then should you leave the proposal with them.

Also be sure to ask when you might expect an answer!! When you return from your visit be sure to write a brief letter thanking the Foundation for the opportunity to visit and for their consideration of your request.

5. **NO Visit**: If the foundation is not easily visited, or they indicate that a visit isn't necessary, then determine their interest and send the proposal with an appropriate cover letter thanking them for their consideration of your request. Make sure you specify in the letter the amount of the request and a brief summary statement of the problem, the project, the need and what their grant will accomplish. Point out the enclosed Case for Support (again, if you have one) and detail the specific area for which the request is being made.

6. **Follow-up Calls**: It is appropriate to make follow up calls to foundations for various reasons...

   a) If you mailed a proposal, then you may call within a week to verify that the foundation received your proposal, and to ask when you might expect to hear an answer to your request.

   b) If you presented your proposal in person during a visit, then you should call about a week before the foundation indicated it will make a decision. This call is to make sure they are still considering your request and to see if they need any further information that will help them make their decision. Thank them once more and indicate that you are looking forward to their reply.

7. **Thank you letters!!** Once you have received a reply you will either be rejoicing that your request has been approved, or you'll be looking for other sources of funding! In either case, be sure to thank the Foundation. In case of a denial, be sure to ask the foundation whether they would consider another submission at a later time.

8. **Record-keeping**: There are many approaches to record-keeping and contact logs, but the fact is that SOME consistent format should be used to document every step you take with all the foundations you contact. Alternatively, your donor management software should provide you with effective "foundations management" tools and procedures. Set up a special file called "Foundation Relations" and resolve to keep track of everything you do with foundations.

   You may make proposals to multiple foundations for the same project. Some of your programs or projects may be appropriate for proposals to churches. In this case, you should run the process in much the same manner as described above – assuming that your guidelines permit you to approach churches. You should also set up a special file for "Church Relations" and use the same type of forms as for the foundations.

The Foundation File

1) The following information should be recorded and appear in the file:

   - The full, correct name of the foundation
   - Precise street address and phone number (website, if available)
   - Officers or directors and their professional connections

- Brief historical sketch -- when founded, by whom, for what purpose
- Current assets
- Amount and number of recent grants -- by year and by individual recipient
- High, low, average and suggested "first time awards" if available
- Pattern of giving -- to what kind of institutions, for what purposes, etc.
- Contact people -- if specified, or best guess until confirmed via contact
- Any organizational connections with foundation (i.e. board member contacts, golfing partners, friends of friends, etc.)?
- History of your organization's contact / grants from foundation
- Recent 990 with income and grants made
- Guidelines, schedules, process, areas of limitation
- Most recent annual report if available

2) Also included should be a contact log recording every interaction / communication with the foundation, by whom, date, purpose and specific outcome (if any). Most donor software permits this type of log to be created for ALL contacts/records on your database. Be sure to code all foundations as "foundations" so the computer can easily generate reports, contact logs, etc. "on demand" so you have easy access to this vital information!

3) Copies of (meaningful) correspondence, such as submissions, proposals, etc.

Foundation Reports

Your donor management software can likely provide a variety of reports that will help track progress with foundations, both for contact and foundation relationship management and for tracking financial performance. These include the following types:

Action Reports:

1. Tickler and Action Detail Report
2. Action Summary Reports

Profiles, Lists and Directory Reports:

1. Constituent Directory
2. Organization / Constituent Profile

Financial Reports:

1. Constituent Giving History

Analytical Reports:

1. Solicitor Goal Summary
2. Solicitor Performance Reports
3. First/Greatest/Latest Report
4. LYBUNT Report (Last Year But Unfortunately Not This)
5. Top Donors Report

In Conclusion...

The time, effort and energy that go into a successful Foundations Program are considerable – but they are worth it. Like everything in development, you must simply remember that there is no big, easy or fast solution to your funding needs. With foundations, that is especially true.

Remember that you must get in line, stay in line, get to the head of the line, then get back in line.

Here's hoping you achieve success!

About the Author...

Jeff McLinden has had a varied career in broadcasting, advertising, private Christian education and many opportunities to serve in Christian ministry. He has worked in the areas of resource development and marketing for nonprofit institutions since 1979 including senior roles in development, creative marketing and management for Campus Crusade for Christ, The Christian Broadcasting Network, and Bible Literature International.

In 1988, Jeff was awarded recognition for exemplary service as a Development Professional by the Development Association for Christian Institutions (DACI). He spent 20 years as a vice president with McConkey-Johnston International, a consulting firm that specializes in helping nonprofit organizations in areas of management, marketing, organizational development and resource development. After joining the M/J team in 1992, Jeff helped a broad variety of clients in many areas of fundraising, donor and missionary resource development, marketing, communications and organizational change. He specializes in marketing and development communications strategies, such as direct mail fundraising, development publications, and the creation and management of donor membership and involvement programs, and is a frequent speaker and leader of seminars on these topics at professional development conferences across North America. He is also the founder of Raising-Support.com, an online resource and training center for missionaries and others who must raise personal support for their work. And in 2008, Jeff started his own company, Wordsmith Marketing, LLC that specializes in Branding, Internet Marketing and Communications strategies for nonprofit organizations. You can visit his website here: http://wordsmith-marketing.com.

www.ingramcontent.com/pod-product-compliance
Lightning Source LLC
Chambersburg PA
CBHW051737170526
45167CB00002B/966